Grandma MarGtie'S Tale of The WiSe Young SaVior

Writer:Dr.K.T. Zulkowski

Illustrator:Marina Trapanese

Published by Mz. Kim Productions

4263 Tierra Rejada Rd #151

Moorpark, CA 93021

www.mzkimproductions.com

ISBN: 978-1-962106-05-4

Printed in United States of America

First Printing: August 2023

Date of Copyright: July 5, 2023

Cover design by Marina Trapanese

Illustrations by Marina Trapanese

Edited by Joshua Nickel

For permissions, please contact: Mz. Kim Productions

4263 Tierra Rejada Rd #151

Moorpark, CA 93021

www.mzkimproductions.com

mzkimproductions@gmail.com

Dedication:

To all young people seeking to teach others about their savior, This book is dedicated to you. May you be filled with a deep desire to learn and understand God's Word, just like Jesus did. May you find joy in sharing His wisdom with others and may you inspire those around you to grow in their faith. May Grandma Margie's Tale of the Wise Young Savior serve as a reminder of the importance of seeking knowledge and understanding, regardless of age. May it encourage you to ask questions, listen, and learn from those who have wisdom to share. May you be like Zipporah and Zion, eager and curious to hear the stories of Jesus and to grow in wisdom and stature. May you be like Jesus, displaying a love for God's Word and a desire to share His teachings with others. This book is dedicated to all young people who are on a journey of faith and discovery. May you find inspiration and guidance in the story of Jesus teaching in the temple, and may it strengthen your commitment to spreading His love and wisdom to those around you.

With love and blessings,
Dr. K.T. Zulkowski

1. Hear the Gospel. (Romans 10:17, John 8:32)
2. Believe the Gospel (Hebrews 11:6, John 20:31)
3. Repent of past sins (Luke 13:3, Acts 17:30)
4. Confess faith in Jesus Christ (Romans 10:10, Matthew 10:32)
5. Be Baptized (Galatians 3:27, Mark 16:16,
Acts 2:38)
6. Be faithful unto death (Revelation 2:10)

Author's Note:

Dear Reader, Thank you for embarking on this journey with me through Grandma Margie's Tale of the Wise Young Savior. It is my hope that this story will inspire and encourage young people in their faith and their desire to teach others about their savior. As a writer, I am passionate about creating stories that not only entertain but also impart valuable lessons and teachings. The story of Jesus teaching in the temple as a young boy is one that has always fascinated me, and I wanted to bring it to life in a way that would resonate with young readers. In Grandma Margie, I have sought to create a character who embodies wisdom, love, and a deep understanding of God's Word. She serves as a guide and mentor for Zipporah and Zion, showing them the importance of seeking knowledge and sharing it with others. Through this story, I hope to convey the message that age is not a barrier to wisdom and teaching. Like Jesus, who amazed the teachers in the temple with His understanding and answers, young people have the ability to inspire and teach others through their knowledge and love for God's Word. I also hope to encourage young readers to have a thirst for knowledge and a desire to grow in wisdom, just as Jesus did. Learning and understanding God's Word is a lifelong journey, and it is my hope that this book will ignite a passion for studying and sharing His teachings. Lastly, I want to express my gratitude to all the young people who have a heart for teaching others about their savior. Your dedication and enthusiasm are truly inspiring. May this book serve as a reminder of the importance of your mission and may it empower you to continue spreading the love and wisdom of Jesus to those around you. Thank you for joining me on this adventure. I hope that Grandma Margie's Tale of the Wise Young Savior will leave a lasting impact on your heart and encourage you to embrace your role as a teacher and ambassador for Christ.

With love and blessings,
Dr. K.T. Zulkowski

Educational Value:

The educational value of the book "Grandma Margie's Tale of the Wise Young Savior" is to teach children about the wisdom and knowledge of Jesus as a young boy. It introduces the concept of Jesus' understanding of God's Word and his ability to teach and answer questions. The book also emphasizes the importance of learning and growing in wisdom, encouraging children to study and understand God's Word like Jesus did. Overall, the book aims to inspire children to develop a love for learning and a desire to deepen their understanding of spirituality. In addition to teaching children about the wisdom and knowledge of Jesus, "Grandma Margie's Tale of the Wise Young Savior" also has several other educational values: 1. Cultural and Historical Understanding: The book introduces children to the setting of the temple and the significance of Jesus' presence there. It provides a glimpse into the cultural and historical context of Jesus' time, helping children develop a better understanding of biblical events. 2. Scripture Knowledge: Throughout the book, Grandma Margie quotes scripture from the Bible, specifically from the book of Luke. This helps children become familiar with biblical passages and encourages them to engage with the text. 3. Critical Thinking and Questioning: The book highlights Jesus' ability to ask questions and engage in thoughtful discussions with the teachers in the temple. This can inspire children to develop their own critical thinking skills and encourages them to ask questions and seek knowledge. 4. Character Development: The book emphasizes the virtues of wisdom, humility, and love for God's Word. Through the story, children can learn about the importance of these qualities and how they can apply them in their own lives. 5. Family Bonding and Storytelling: The book portrays a warm and inviting atmosphere with Grandma Margie sharing a story with her grandchildren. This can encourage a love for storytelling and family bonding, as well as inspire children to learn from their elders and value their wisdom. Overall, "Grandma Margie's Tale of the Wise Young Savior" offers educational value by teaching children about Jesus' wisdom, promoting scripture knowledge, fostering critical thinking, encouraging character development, and emphasizing the importance of family and storytelling. Perfect for children any age this book is an invaluable resource for parents, grandparents, and educators who wish to introduce young minds to the wonders of the Bible. It fosters a love for reading, a curiosity for learning, and a strong foundation of faith that will accompany children throughout their lives.

Grandma Margie's Tale of The WiSe Young SaVior

Grandma Margie: *Once upon a time, my dear Zipporah and Zion, there was a young boy named Jesus who went on an incredible adventure!*

Grandma Margie: *This is the temple, a special place where people went to worship God.*
Jesus and his family visited the temple every year.

4

Zion: *Grandma, why did they go to the temple every year?*
Grandma Margie: *In the Bible, it says that they went to celebrate a special holiday called Passover.*

Zipporah: *Look, Grandma! There's Jesus sitting with the teachers!*
Grandma Margie: *Yes, my dear. Jesus was only twelve years old, but he was already very wise.*

Zion: *What was Jesus doing, Grandma?*
Grandma Margie: *Jesus was listening to the teachers and asking them questions. He wanted to learn more about God and His Word.*

Zipporah: *Grandma, why did Jesus stay behind?*
Grandma Margie: *Well, my sweet Zipporah, Jesus' family left the temple, but Jesus stayed behind without them knowing.*

Zion: *What did Jesus do, Grandma?*
Grandma Margie: *Jesus started teaching the teachers about God's love and His plans for the world. Everyone was amazed by his wisdom!*

Zipporah: *Did Jesus' family know he was missing?*
Grandma Margie: *No, my dear. They were worried and searched for him everywhere.*

Zion: *Did they find Jesus, Grandma?*
Grandma Margie: *Yes, after three days of searching, they found Jesus in the temple, talking with the teachers.*

Zipporah: *Were they angry with Jesus?*
Grandma Margie: *At first, they were worried, but when they saw Jesus, they were relieved.*
Mary said, "Son, why have you done this to us? We were so worried!"

Zipporah: *Did Jesus go home with his family?*
Grandma Margie: *Yes, my dear. Jesus went back home with Mary and Joseph, and he continued to grow in wisdom and favor with God and people.*

Zion: *Grandma, why is this story important?*
Grandma Margie: *This story shows us that even at a young age, Jesus knew his purpose was to teach others about God's love and His plans for the world.*

Zipporah: *Grandma, can we read more about Jesus in the Bible?*

Grandma Margie: *Absolutely, my dear! In the book of Luke, chapter 2, you can find this amazing story and many more about Jesus.*

Zion: *Grandma, I want to learn more about God like Jesus did!*

Grandma Margie: *That's wonderful, my dear Zion! Let's explore the Bible together and discover the amazing things God has in store for us.*

Zipporah: *Grandma, can we visit the temple like Jesus did?*

Grandma Margie: *Of course, my sweet Zipporah! We can visit the temple and worship God, just like Jesus and his family did.*

Zion: *Grandma, I feel closer to God here!*
Grandma Margie: *That's because the temple is a special place where we can connect with God and learn more about His love.*

Zipporah: *Grandma, can we pray like Jesus did?*
Grandma Margie: *Absolutely, my dear! Let's pray together and talk to God, just like Jesus.*

Zion: *Grandma, how can we be wise like Jesus?*
Grandma Margie: *We can be wise by studying God's Word, just like Jesus did in the temple. The Bible is full of wisdom and guidance for our lives.*

Zipporah: *Grandma, can we share what we learn with others, just like Jesus did?*

Grandma Margie: *Absolutely, my dear! We can share God's love and teachings with our friends and family, just like Jesus did with the teachers in the temple.*

Zion: *Grandma, I want to be brave like Jesus!*
Grandma Margie: *That's wonderful, my brave Zion!*
With God's help, we can be courageous and stand up
for what is right, just like Jesus did.

Zipporah: *Grandma, can we help others like Jesus did?*
Grandma Margie: *Absolutely, my dear! We can show kindness and love to those in need, just like Jesus did throughout his life.*

Zion: *Grandma, I want to follow Jesus just like you!*
Grandma Margie: *That fills my heart with joy, my dear Zion! Let's continue to learn from Jesus' example and follow Him with all our hearts.*

Grandma Margie: *And so, my dear Zipporah and Zion, the story of young Jesus in the temple teaches us about the importance of seeking wisdom, sharing God's love, and following Jesus' footsteps. Remember, God has a special plan for each one of us!*

The End

www.ingramcontent.com/pod-product-compliance
Lightning Source LLC
Chambersburg PA
CBHW041524120626
46551CB00018B/2555